Day.
An Organ   ...nual

Praise for the program

"The Days of Respect experience was truly riveting. Trying to establish a common ground between different ethnicities, genders, and sexes proved to be a beneficial task. In order for our society to accept and understand diversity, programs such as Days of Respect are essential."

— Devon Franklin, a senior at Albany High School (the first school to implement the Days of Respect program)

"Once again, the Oakland Men's Project leads the way in our field in creating a thoughtful, sensitive, and user-friendly curriculum. Its comprehensive approach helps young people deal with the deeper, more sensitive issues around violence in a caring, safe, and respectful manner. A wonderful, needed addition to the field of violence prevention."

— Linda Lantieri, National Director, Resolving Conflict Creatively Program and co-author of *Waging Peace in our Schools*

Days of Respect Received an Award of Excellence from the California School Board Association

About the Days of Respect Program

The Days of Respect program was developed by Ralph J. Cantor, a high school teacher and counselor for over twenty-five years who holds master's degrees in teaching and counseling. He directed the Student Assistance Program at Albany High School, is an educational trainer for Far West Laboratories in San Francisco, and directs Innovations in Learning, a private educational consulting firm. Days of Respect has been cited for excellence with an award from the California School Board Association. If you wish information, assistance, or training in the implementation of a Days of Respect program, please contact

Ralph J. Cantor
Innovations in Learning
2808 Hillegass Avenue
Berkeley, CA 94705
(510) 845-9494

About the Oakland Men's Project

The Oakland Men's Project, a community prevention and training program focused on issues of interpersonal violence, is nationally recognized for its trainings and curricula, including *Helping Teens Stop Violence: A Practical Guide for Parents, Counselors, and Educators* (Alameda, CA: Hunter House, 1992) and *Young Men's Work: Building Skills to Stop Violence* (Center City, MN: Hazelden, 1995), a ten-session group curriculum. The Days of Respect program was inspired by workshops conducted at Albany High School in Albany, California, in 1992 and coordinated by Heru-Nefera Amen, the director of youth programming at the Oakland Men's Project. OMP may be reached at

Oakland Men's Project
1203 Preservation Park Way, Suite 200
Oakland, CA 93612
(510) 835-2433
Fax: (510) 835-2466

Organizing A Schoolwide Violence Prevention Program

Ralph Cantor with Paul Kivel, Allan Creighton and the Oakland Men's Project

Hunter House Inc., Publishers
An imprint of Turner Publishing Company
Nashville, Tennessee
www.turnerpublishing.com

Various exercises (Agreements: p. 32; Stand-Up: pp. 47–48) adapted from *Helping Teens Stop
Violence: A Practical Guide for Counselors, Educators and Parents* by Allan Creighton with Paul Kivel,
©1992 Allan Creighton, Battered Women's Alternatives, the Oakland Men's Project. Used with
permission from Hunter House Inc., Alameda, CA (800) 266-5592.

Library of Congress Cataloging-in-Publication Data

Days of Respect: organizing a schoolwide violence prevention program / Ralph Cantor . . . [et al.].
—1st ed.
p. cm. — (Making the Peace)
Includes bibliographical references.
ISBN 0-89793-206-4 (pbk.)
1. Days of Respect (Program) 2. School violence—United States—Prevention.

I. Cantor, Ralph, 1944–   . II. Series.
LB3013.3.D395   1996   371.5'8—dc20   96-34128   CIP

Cover Design and Logo: Jil Weil, Oakland
Book design: Janet Wood
Project Editors: Lisa E. Lee, Jane E. Moore
Marketing: Corrine M. Sahli
Customer Support: Sharon R.A. Olson, Edgar M. Estavilla, Jr., A & A Quality Shipping
Publisher: Kiran S. Rana

Logo 3-D fimo illustration: Christine Benjamin
Production: Paul J. Frindt, Kiran S. Rana
Development/Copyediting: Mali Apple
Promotion & Publicity: Kim A. Wallace

Printed in the United States of America
9   8   7   6   5   4   First edition

List of Contents

Acknowledgments

"I wish to thank Devon Franklin and Amy Johnson, students; Pat Mullarkey and Sally Outis, parents; and Bob Allegrotti, teacher. Without their help, Days of Respect would not have been a success."

— Ralph Cantor

About the cover design

When I was given the job of designing an identity for the Making the Peace project, I sat and thought of possible imagery to represent violence prevention. Many negative images came to my mind—guns, drugs, peer pressure, hate—all things that today's young people have to deal with in their lives. However, none of these carried the message that I wanted to send: hope. So I sat and thought some more, and came up with the image of a patchwork quilt, a traditional American art. But I wanted to create a patchwork that was really American, for today. I researched different traditional designs and folk art, and a design gradually evolved that was made up of ethnic patterns and symbols that represent the diversity that makes up America. While each pattern is exciting and unique on its own, together they make something beautiful that is even stronger. And yet you can see how close some of these original folk designs are to each other. So my design celebrates diversity, and it celebrates unity, because I believe it is the combination of these two things that make a country truly great.

— Jil Weil, Oakland, California

Introduction to the Days of Respect Program

Martin Luther King Jr. once defined violence as "whatever denies human integrity, and leads to hopelessness and helplessness." Under this broad definition, every day in most schools in the United States is a day of violence—a day when a few or many students, teachers, staff members, or parents are ignored, belittled, called a name, harassed, discriminated against, threatened, assaulted, wounded, or even killed.

What would a day of *respect* be like? Any member of a school community can answer this question at once: a day of mutual care and regard, dignity, physical and emotional safety; a day when everyone counts, and everyone counts upon everyone else.

This is the mission of the Days of Respect program: a collaboration of students, parents, and teachers working together to end verbal, emotional, sexual, and physical harassment and abuse in the campus community by making the peace. The program builds a cooperative community by bringing young people and adults together to meet, to plan, to train each other, and finally to facilitate a multiday, schoolwide Days of Respect event.

This culminating, schoolwide event gives public voice to every member of the school community. It suspends the ordinary business of the school and gives every school member a day in which to think about, experience, and practice respect.

The day begins with an assembly organized by young people and adults using skits, videos, musical performances, poetry, dance, and personal testimony to identify—in clear and dramatic terms—the problems of violence and the need all young people have for respect. After the assembly, students gather in small groups, diverse by gender, race, and age, to discuss and speak out on the issues raised in the assembly, under the guidance of student/teacher/parent facilitator teams. All participants then reassemble to speak at an open microphone about what they have learned and experienced. Students and adults make follow-up plans based on the insights, energy, and commitments generated among students and parents during the event.

The Need for Respect

The word *respect* can be loosely defined as mutual care and regard, dignity, and physical and emotional safety; a state in which everyone counts, and everyone counts upon everyone else. Respect is a quality that we can all define for ourselves—and we all know when we are receiving it, and when we aren't.

Young people experience disrespect and outright abuse routinely in our society. Many live with day-to-day anger, frustration, disappointment, or hopelessness about the limits set on them in their adult-defined world. Their responses to these feelings range from passivity to self-destructive behavior, from rude comebacks to picking up a weapon for a counterattack. Some youth feel that the only way to regain self-respect is to demonstrate that they are strong, tough, and unfeeling—to earn respect by beating it out of others. There is so little respect around that it seems like a zero-sum game: to have some myself, I must take it from you. This attempt at recognition, based on a disrespect of others, actually decreases the safety, well-being, self-regard, and respect from others for which young people long.

Respect is not a zero-sum game. A world that respects young people routinely *increases* self-respect and one's ability to respect others. Students who have self-respect and respect for others are resilient to disrespect or abuse, and are less likely to be disrespectful or abusive in their attitudes, comments, and behavior. In an environment of respect, young people are free to embrace the educational process.

What is the origin of the climate of disrespect among young people? Obviously, young people will always be vulnerable to disrespect in a world in which as a group they have less power, fewer resources, and less control over their lives than adults. But that world is also marked by other power inequities that bring about disrespect and violence. Poverty, racism, male gender-role training, economic dislocation, sexism, and cultural norms that extol wealth, physical power, guns, and control are some of the causes—and effects—of violence in our society. All of them foster the climate of disrespect; all of them teach young people that the only way they can gain respect is at the expense of others.

The Making the Peace curriculum explores the issues surrounding violence and its causes in a fifteen-session format. The Days of Respect program speaks to students' immediate need for recognition, participation, respect, and connection. It is a forum in which students can begin the process of understanding, intervening in, and preventing the root causes of violence.

The Goals of the Days of Respect Program

The main purpose of the Days of Respect program is to enable the educational process of a campus community to flourish. To achieve this, the program goals are

- to enlist and prepare students to become leaders in building a schoolwide climate of respect
- to engage and mobilize every student to build respect and to decrease violence
- to develop active family and community participation with students in building respect
- to sustain an annual Days of Respect program
- to establish a permanent, collaborative, democratic problem-solving and violence-reduction process within the school that involves students, teachers, parents, and administrators

In the long term, the program will result in reduced violence and increased safety within the school community.

The Days of Respect program achieves these goals by cultivating a schoolwide commitment to respectful behavior—behavior that promotes everyone's integrity, safety, and well-being. Respectful behavior is marked by the acknowledgment and valuing of racial, gender, age, and other differences; the practice of listening to others; the willingness to make and honor agreements for mutual respect; and the ability to solve problems and make decisions cooperatively.

The Role of Young People

Students are key to the Days of Respect program. They are expected and encouraged to take leadership in all parts of the work. The program is based on the assumption that students, with adult support, can identify and solve the problems they face at school—that they are prepared to take responsibility for themselves, the program, and the school community. It builds on students' strengths and resiliency, including their knowledge of the school community, their facility in expressing their feelings, their capacity for critical thinking, and their ability to work together to find solutions to community problems.

The Days of Respect program operates by combining the leadership abilities of students representing every constituency on campus: every cultural and economic group, both genders, all age levels, and students on both the traditional inside and the traditional outside of campus systems. An explicit purpose of the program is to train these youth to welcome and represent their differences and to share leadership in creating the school atmosphere they want.

The program is based on the premise that students have different learning styles. The experiential nature and varying formats of the activities invite the involvement of all students. The multimedia assembly draws on students' creative abilities to develop effective ways to communicate with one another.

Adults and Young People in Collaboration

The Days of Respect program is built on collaboration. At every stage of the program students, parents, staff, and teachers work together, practicing and modeling collaborative problem solving. Parents are given an opportunity to become more connected with the school, and students, parents, and teachers have a chance to relate to each other in new, more respectful and productive ways. The collaborative learning process of putting the program together is as important as the culminating event.

In addition, students and parents are engaged because each group knows that its interests and perspectives are represented. Representatives from both groups are involved from the initial stages of the program and function as equal collaborators in its development.

All the information you need to run a Days of Respect program is included in this manual. All the energy, enthusiasm, and creativity for making the program a success can be found in your school. Your leadership is the vital link that will connect the program to the school and make it a place where respect is practiced, day by day.

Becoming a Days of Respect Organizer

To organize means, among other things, to connect; to bring all parts into a whole; to combine the power of several small movements into one mighty action; and to enable a gathering of people to see, experience, and activate itself as a community. Organizing is different from teaching, counseling, facilitating, and administering.

As an organizer of a Days of Respect program on your campus, you take responsibility for the process from beginning to end. You will need to attend to many details. You will have to create a specific step-by-step plan that will be accessible to and understood by others. Much of what you do will be in front of others; much will be behind the scenes. Not the least of your tasks is enabling others to share that responsibility. Almost the first step this guide suggests, you will notice, is enlisting a co-organizer.

You, as organizer, agree to hold out a vision of a community imbued with respect, and you become responsible for working toward that vision through respectful means, modeling the climate and atmosphere you are helping to create. Your interaction with all the other leaders who will step forth is crucial—because your relationships with them will model the mutual respect you wish to promote at the school. And, finally, what you do must be doable by others. The ultimate goal of organizing such a program is to make room for people to take your place; this may be your most visible sign of success. This is the time, before you begin, to think about what you as an organizer will need.

Before You Begin

You are a teacher, counselor, student, parent, administrator, or community or agency member associated with a school. What will you need to undertake a Days of Respect program?

Take some time to identify your allies in or outside your school community, people who are ready simply to listen to you or to support you as you work your way through this process. Consider whether you might benefit from gathering information or securing training on topics such as understanding abuse and violence, multicultural diversity, facilitating groups, or working with the media.

Take some time to consider the Agreements (see page 32), the working guidelines this program uses for members of a group to govern their interactions with respect. Think practically about what *your* list of agreements would be, and what agreements would fit the members of your campus community. Practice explaining them to people and encouraging people to use them with each other. Consider how to bring all the students on your campus into a working knowledge and use of these agreements with each other.

The Agreements are published in *Making the Peace: A 15-Session Violence Prevention Curriculum for Young People* (P. Kivel et al., Hunter House Inc., Publishers, Alameda CA, 1997). The Days of Respect program is designed to be self-contained, but you may wish to obtain a copy of *Making the Peace* to examine the context in which the Agreements are used in the classroom. The curriculum explores the root causes of violence across lines of gender, race, economic class, and age, with exercises and activities used to train young people to make the peace. It presents our best understanding of how young people and adults can act as allies in stopping violence. We strongly believe that genuine respect among students can only be secured when the dynamics of the power imbalances of age, gender, and race are addressed.

You can use *Making the Peace* to prepare yourself for working with these issues. You might use some of the exercises in your work with youth, or take a class of young people through the entire curriculum as a preparation for initiating a Days of Respect program with their help. The bibliography in that work lists curricula, articles, books, and other resources you may find useful in working with youth.

Finally, we encourage you to sit quietly for a few minutes to envision, in detail, your school operating day to day in a state of full respect. What would it look like? How would the classes operate? What would the corridors look like between classes? What will you see on the school grounds before, during, and at the end of the day? How will it be for you to work there? How will it look when everyone is included, proudly representing their own groups and actively engaged in building alliances? How will your campus operate when everyone truly counts, and everyone counts upon everyone else? This is the vision with which you will begin.

Funding

The Days of Respect program is designed for junior high, middle, and high schools, private and continuation schools, and small colleges, all of which have tight budgets and few extra resources. Planned and implemented mainly by student and parent volunteers, it demands relatively little time commitment from school staff or expense to the school district. The program takes two to three months to implement and is structured for approximately eight required meetings. The program provides a framework for cooperation, generates enthusiasm, trains facilitators, gets tasks assigned, and then lets the participants work independently.

The primary expense of the program is payment of the organizers. While most of the tasks involved in mounting a Days of Respect program can be accomplished by volunteers, there will be one or more people whose level of commitment and responsibility to the project should be compensated. Sources of these minimal funds might be the school budget, the PTA, local businesses, local foundations, fundraisers or special events, or special state and federal funds for violence prevention, substance abuse prevention, or school improvement.

Media Involvement

Media coverage of education—particularly the less sensationalized, more positive aspects of what young people do—is inadequate and sorely needed. Young people need to see positive images of themselves and models of other youth involved in constructive social action. Adults need to see more examples of the positive leadership young people take in the struggle to stop violence. A Days of Respect program harnesses the power of publicity to help organize and heighten the effect of the Days of Respect event.

Media coverage is critical: it sends students the important message that their efforts at solving their own problems are acknowledged and supported, and it attracts support for school activities from the wider community. Part of your role will be to establish a partnership with local media by using suggested strategies and guidelines for involving newspaper, radio, and television journalists in the project from the beginning.

The Days of Respect program initiates a long-term process of problem solving and productive change through the active participation of students, parents and teachers, media representatives, and other community members—a school/community collaboration that will attract greater resources to support efforts to reduce violence and to make the peace.

A Few Things to Keep in Mind

Keep the following general principles in mind when organizing a Days of Respect program at your school.

- *When safety is established, participation will follow.* The Days of Respect program creates a safe, structured environment in which all participants can share their hopes and fears, difficulties, and ideas. The exercises are designed to stretch people—and their imaginations. The guidelines for facilitator training ensure creative, productive, and *safe* interactions.

- *Teach cooperation through collaboration.* The collaborative process of creating a Days of Respect event models the process of replacing conflict with cooperation. Participants practice and train others in the skills necessary for peaceful and democratic problem solving.

- *Diversity and differences are strengths to build on, but this process takes time and commitment.* Organizing people with different cultural, racial, and economic backgrounds; genders; ages; modes of learning; and ways of relating takes time. Everyone must be committed to working through their differences to achieve common goals. Drawing upon and celebrating the diverse strengths of each individual is the only effective and long-lasting way to achieve mutual respect.

- *Respect grows from cultural pride and the building of alliances.* Respect develops from listening to others tell their stories and from being listened to and acknowledged by others. The two necessary components of making the peace are taking pride in one's own culture and heritage and a willingness to be an ally to others of different backgrounds. Neither will work in isolation from the other.

- *Real mutual respect requires everyone to recognize and work to reverse systematic injustice.* Systematic injustice and inequality—the one-down status of young people, women, poor people, people of color, immigrants, and many other groups—is built into our society and is the root cause of and context for violence in our schools. This fact must be acknowledged and understood. The Days of Respect program focuses on how we can make peace within a particular context—the school community—by understanding cultural differences and systematic inequities, and by building respect and cooperation among individuals and within the larger school community.*

- *Emphasize the prevention of violence.* A community-strengthening, proactive approach to violence and other problem areas young people face, such as substance abuse and unwanted pregnancy, is more effective and far less costly than punitive or reactive approaches such as metal detectors, discipline measures, incarceration, and other adult-defined strategies.

- *Expect the program to change as it develops.* Organizing an entire community to address the issue of respect is an exercise in continual negotiation, compromise, revision, and recommitment.

- *Expect that you will change.* When you work for full inclusion of all voices, you will learn new things about others and yourself—and unlearn things you believed about both. This may be the most challenging—and certainly one of the most exciting—effects of your, and others', participation in the program.

- *Remember that substantive change occurs over time and is usually initiated by a small group of committed individuals.* The Days of Respect program is the beginning of a process of collaboration and dialogue from which other activities and discussions will follow. It is not necessary to involve all participants, to get everyone's approval, or to have everything planned in advance and all volunteers in line before proceeding with the program.

> *"Never doubt that a small group of committed people can change the world; indeed it is the only thing that ever has."*
>
> — Margaret Mead

---

* For a detailed look at the social roots of violence, see the essays in *Helping Teens Stop Violence* by Allan Creighton with Paul Kivel, Alameda, CA: Hunter House, 1992.

Implementing a Days of Respect Program

- Step 1 — Present the Days of Respect Idea to Administration and Staff

- Step 2 — Choose Organizers and Create a Steering Committee

- Step 3 — Conduct Surveys and Create an Assembly Committee

- Step 4 — Create a Provisional Plan and Begin the Assembly Process

- Step 5 — Conduct a Presentation for Teachers

- Step 6 — Finalize the Plan

- Step 7 — Select Students for the Assembly and Small Groups

- Step 8 — Train the Steering Committee

- Step 9 — Train Facilitators

- Step 10 — Conduct the Days of Respect Event

- Step 11 — Hold a Follow-up Meeting and Make Continuation Plans

Step 1
Present the Days of Respect Idea to Administration and Staff

One or two people who are familiar with the materials in this manual and who are enthusiastic about the program should talk with key administrators and make a short presentation to the staff to get approval to initiate a Days of Respect program. During this presentation, review the goals for the Days of Respect program (see page 3) and include the following points:

- The Days of Respect program is part of a violence prevention strategy.

- The program involves students and fosters student leadership.

- The program brings students, teachers, and parents together to identify and solve school-based problems.

- The program can create favorable local media attention.

- The program requires a minimal investment.

You might want to conduct the stand-up exercise (see pages 47-48) with staff to give them an understanding of the kind of issues raised by the Days of Respect program. If a group of students or a class has used the Making the Peace curriculum, they may want to be involved in initiating the program.

Step 2
Choose Organizers and Create a Steering Committee

Choose Organizers

The organizers (we recommend that two people share the work) are the key motivators of the Days of Respect program. They might be you and a colleague, or you might support another person or persons in this position. The organizers will recruit, train, motivate, and support the students, parents, teachers, and staff involved in the program. Their primary task is to initiate the program and to support the Steering Committee and Assembly Committee in their work. The organizers may be teachers, counselors, special staff, or parents—adults with the time, enthusiasm, and experience to pull the program together. A vice-principal or administrator is also a good candidate. This manual will help to guide him or her through the process of instituting the Days of Respect program at your school.

Create a Steering Committee

The organizers bring together a group of students, faculty, parents, and other members of the community—approximately twenty people in all—to begin planning. This will be the "Steering Committee," the inner circle of engaged participants who will design and carry out all of the program activities to follow. Some of the members of this Steering Committee will also elect to be part of the Assembly Committee. The task of the Steering Committee is to plan and oversee the entire program, and to serve as recruiters from and advocates for their respective constituencies. Along with the organizers, they will conduct the facilitators' training.

As organizers, your first step is to consult with a school administrator, such as a principal or vice-principal, and identify potential Steering Committee members. An administrator, such as a vice-principal, is in fact a crucial member of the steering committee. This person should be allotted time by the school, and then given the responsibility to handle the many logistical tasks necessary to make the project work (see "school administrator" role, page 35). Among these tasks are scheduling meetings, facilitating communication between steering committee members, and preparing meeting space. This is also the person who, for the day(s) of the event, makes task assignments for the entire faculty, chooses the method of selecting and assigning students to small groups to ensure gender and racial balance, and decides how to inform students of their group assignments.

Be sure students, parents, and faculty have ample representation in the planning and implementation phases. Involve key people from the community such as school board members, student government representatives, administrators, PTA officers, teachers, union representatives, guidance counselors, media people, and civic leaders.

Take time to think about the composition of this group, paying attention to cultural, ethnic, age, gender, and community segment balance. Expect that you will need to make a special effort to encourage some people to be part of the group and to ensure that the group is accessible and safe enough for everyone. It is especially important to think about how to represent youth opinion leaders (young people others look up to) who are outside the campus mainstream, different from youth who are in student government or are high academic achievers. You will also want to choose students and adults who are excited about the program, who can work together in a group, and who have a positive attitude about the possibility of making changes in the school environment.

Next, send a letter to potential members, and follow up with a telephone call or in person to explain more about the Days of Respect program and its goals, with an invitation to attend an orientation meeting. See the sample welcoming letter to Steering Committee members on page 33.

You will probably need to hold at least five Steering Committee meetings to get the Days of Respect program up and running. Follow these guidelines for facilitating the Steering Committee meetings:

- *Establish a clear set of agreements about how people will work with one another, and model the process you expect of participants.*
  Respect is built upon people honoring agreements. Establish your agreements (our suggested list is on page 32) at the opening meeting, and review them at each subsequent meeting. Make sure people follow through on commitments, show up on time, and are listened to. Help people focus on the goals of the program rather than on personality differences. Discuss from the start the need to practice tolerance for the differences in how people operate and communicate.

- *Be flexible and sensitive to the needs of the group.* Part of your role as an organizer is to pay attention to the group process and to the group as a whole. When a relatively large group of diverse people works together, things don't always go smoothly. Everyone needs an opportunity to express her or his concerns and ideas. As you don't want the meetings to go much beyond two hours, you may need to hold an extra meeting or two before the Steering Committee training session, which is scheduled for the fifth meeting. Delegate responsibility and involve others as much as possible in these tasks and decisions.

- *Acknowledge from the start the views of those who oppose implementing the Days of Respect program.* You will undoubtedly encounter people who will not want to participate or who are threatened by change. As an organizer, you need to accept all views and allow people who want to make change to take leadership roles.

- *Keep the workload of teachers and staff at a minimum, except for those who really want to be involved.* Be clear about job assignments. Make sure each person knows his or her assignment and has the resources to complete it; see the list of Steering Committee roles on page 35.

- *Build in media involvement.* Involving the media in the process from the start—as reporters, advocates, and supporters—lets students know that what they are doing is important and is being taken seriously. In addition, gaining new understanding of the way in which media covers education and youth issues can impress upon students the idea that media is interactive and that they can have an influence on its content.

- *Build in assessment and evaluation as an organizing component.* Accurately assessing the need for this program will help garner early support and make the activities planned more effective. Proving that the Days of Respect program creates positive change can help fuel enthusiasm and commitment for subsequent activities. All youth and adult leaders can use assessment and evaluation tools to adapt, change, and sharpen their work. See the sample survey and evaluation forms on pages 52–55.

- *Remember that the guidelines in this manual are suggestions.* The final Days of Respect event is a group effort involving all members of the Steering Committee, the Assembly Committee, and the school community. The particular program form and content should be created to respond to the needs of your school.

  For example, in one school, the Steering Committee decided they needed a three-hour workshop that focused just on the relations between students and staff. In another school, it turned out that because of many unresolved conflicts, the Steering Committee—consisting of staff, students, and parents—was not ready to plan a Days of Respect together. Facilitation of issues among Steering Committee members is the first step in creating a Days of Respect program. It is the responsibility of the Steering Committee to plan activities that are appropriate to the particular school site.

Conduct Surveys and Create an Assembly Committee

First Steering Committee Meeting

The first meeting will ensure that everyone in the Steering Committee

— shares and is committed to a vision of the program

— is knowledgeable about the program

— is enthusiastic about the possibilities

— is committed to the agreements for working together

— is taking the first steps to organize the program

Subsequent meetings coordinate events and lay the groundwork for the Steering Committee training, the facilitators' training, and the school-wide Days of Respect event.

The major goals of the first meeting are to develop surveys to assess what has been happening at the school and to set up the Assembly Committee. You will also draft a provisional plan for the Days of Respect program, to be completed at the second Steering Committee meeting.

Agenda for the First Steering Committee Meeting

1. Conduct introductions. Allow each person in the group to say their name and how they are connected to the school. Identify who is a Steering Committee member and who is a visitor or other participant in the program (such as an administrator or media person).

2. Conduct the team-building exercise called "Yes, and. . . ." The group makes a circle, and invents a common project, something imaginary the group will build, for example, a car. The first person suggests a feature that she wants on the car: "It's got to have gold windshield wipers." The second person enthusiastically affirms what the first person said, and adds what he wants: "Yes! and it must have _____ (e.g., eight stereo speakers). Each person completes a "Yes! and _____" until everyone has had a turn.

3. Present an overview of the goals and general structure of the Days of Respect program, answering any questions participants may have.

4. Discuss the teacher and student surveys and organize volunteers to conduct them. Distribute copies of the sample

surveys on pages 52–54. Explain that the surveys will be conducted to get an accurate picture of what kinds of violence and disruptive behavior are prevalent at the school. The results will be used to guide the design of the Days of Respect and to judge its effectiveness. Enlist volunteers to modify the surveys if necessary and to conduct the surveys by the next Steering Committee meeting.

5. Discuss the Days of Respect program and the Assembly Committee. Discuss possible agendas for the Days of Respect program at your school and decide on a provisional plan for the program. Explain the purpose and responsibilities of the Assembly Committee, and enlist volunteers to get it started (the Assembly Committee is described below). Non–Steering Committee members are also needed to participate on this committee.

6. Assign Steering Committee roles, such as committee chairs. Distribute copies of the essential Steering Committee roles (see page 35), and assign the roles as a group. Ask for or appoint volunteers to:

    a. Assembly committee

    b. Media commitee

    c. Recruiting committee for students and parents

    Steering Committee members are asked to volunteer to be committee chairs or co-chairs.

7. Schedule all meeting dates, and review the remaining steps for implementing the Days of Respect program (Steps 4–11).

Follow-up to the First Steering Committee Meeting

After the meeting, the volunteers will conduct the surveys and the Assembly Committee will begin planning the assembly segment of the Days of Respect event.

Conduct Surveys

Conducting the student and teacher surveys can be the first act of building respect—just by raising the issues, you will have begun the process. The volunteers who have agreed to conduct the surveys can adapt the sample student and teacher surveys on pages 52–54 to the needs of your school. All teachers and at least three classes from each grade level should be surveyed. Surveys can be compiled by hand or by using electronic scorers.

Create an Assembly Committee

The Assembly Committee will begin planning the assembly segment of the Days of Respect event. Consisting of students, teachers, and parents, the Assembly Committee will organize the logistics for the assembly and help work with students on presentations for it. English and drama teachers are often good resources for this committee.

Using the sample Days of Respect schedule of events on pages 42–43 and the guidelines for the Days of Respect assembly on page 44, the Assembly Committee will develop an assembly format that harnesses the creativity of the students and the outside community to make the event inspiring, fun, and effective. The committee will present a run-through of the assembly for the facilitators' training (see Step 8), and then conduct the schoolwide assembly as many times as are scheduled. Encourage Assembly Committee members to come to the second Steering Committee meeting for an orientation to the program and to firm up the theme and focus of the assembly.

Guidelines for the Days of Respect Assembly

In general, encourage students to take leadership in putting together the program. The goal of the performance part of the assembly is to show a diverse group of students actually leading the process, to engage *all* students in the enterprise of building respect, and to set the stage for them to speak out in the follow-up sessions. The assembly is not a talent show; you do not need to schedule lots of performance time. The performances themselves should not outshine or distract from the other parts of the program.

Select students to perform a skit, sing a song or a rap, or read a poem that speaks to the issues of respect and problem solving at your school. If a class or group has used the Making the Peace curriculum, there may be students already inspired to express their ideas on this subject. If you have a drama department, its students may also be excited about creating or performing something for the student body. An essay contest on the theme sponsored by the English Department, poster projects sponsored by art teachers, a chorus presentation for the assembly, or a group of students talking about their experiences with the Making the Peace curriculum are just a few of many possible ways to enhance the assembly.

It is also powerful to find a local speaker to address the assembly (for approximately ten minutes), someone effective in speaking to youth who has a relevant experience to relate. Someone who is known to the students is best, but anyone who can generate interest is fine. There are also short videos available that speak to these issues.

Create a Provisional Plan and Begin the Assembly Process

Second Steering Committee Meeting

The major goals of the second meeting are to evaluate the results of the surveys and to develop a theme, focus, and provisional plan for the Days of Respect program. The Steering Committee should be able to complete the provisional plan by the end of the meeting.

Agenda for the Second Steering Committee Meeting

1. Conduct an introduction and icebreaker. Have all participants introduce themselves. Lead a short icebreaker (see glossary) to get people relaxed and working together.

2. Evaluate survey results. Have the volunteers who conducted the survey present their results. As a group, discuss the implications of the results for the Days of Respect program.

3. Review the provisional plan for the Days of Respect program created during the first meeting. Make changes as decided upon by the group.

4. Establish the theme and focus of the program. Choose a name and theme for the program. "Days of Respect" can be used as both if no other ideas are more appropriate for your school and its particular issues.

5. Distribute and review the descriptions of the five small-group exercises on pages 46–51. Talk about the small-group exercises briefly so that Steering Committee members have an idea of what will be happening, besides the assembly, during the Days of Respect event.

6. Establish the focus of the Assembly Committee. With the above discussion in mind, talk about the focus of the Assembly Committee so that the entire group agrees on how the Steering Committee and the Assembly Committee will work together and what each group's emphasis will be. From this point on, the Assembly Committee will work primarily on its own, periodically reporting back to the Steering Committee.

7. Discuss the additional activities. Hold a short discussion of any supplementary activities the Assembly Committee wants to encourage that support the main theme of the Days of Respect program.

8. Develop a strategy for getting media coverage. With the theme and focus chosen, now is the time to bring in media

coverage of the project. Ask for a volunteer to be a media outreach facilitator (see page 35) to draw up lists of potential media contacts, to put together a press release (distribute the guidelines on page 36), and to encourage local press to pay attention to the project. This person, with other volunteers, will form a media outreach subcommittee to connect with student in-school media as well as public media. Personal contact with radio and television reporters and newspaper journalists is invaluable; the subcommittee should solicit ideas for contacts from teachers, staff, and parents.

Remind the media subcommittee not to be discouraged if there is initially not much response. Encourage them to be persistent and to keep the press informed of the progress of the program, providing them with ample notice of the Days of Respect event so that they can attend. The media subcommittee can commend their contacts for helping to counter the usually negative coverage of youth and violence with this example of positive change.

9. Review the remaining steps for implementing the Days of Respect program (Steps 5–11).

Third Steering Committee Meeting

The major goals of the third meeting are to firm up and approve the overall plan for the Days of Respect program, to create a media coverage plan, and to begin the recruitment of facilitators. Optionally, you may want to split this meeting into two meetings, the second one for finalizing the overall plan and filling out final details and responsibilities (see Step 6). The final step in this process will be to train the Steering Committee to lead the small-group exercises and to train the facilitators (see Steps 8 and 9).

Agenda for the Third Steering Committee Meeting

(This agenda for the third meeting can be followed again for additional meetings if they are needed to finalize planning.)

1. Conduct an introduction and icebreaker.

2. Firm up the overall plan for the Days of Respect program. Review the plan as it has been agreed upon to date, including the small-group exercises. A final decision should be made about which exercises to use and how they will be conducted (especially if the exercises will differ from the format suggestions in this manual).

3. Work out the details of the Days of Respect event. The logistics to be resolved might include how students will be selected for the small-group activities, how students will be monitored between parts of the event, how off-campus participants will be directed, how the facilitator teams will be coordinated, what roles the teachers will have, and how supplies will be distributed to the teams. (The administrator should be very involved in this discussion.)

4. Have the Assembly Committee present a progress report. The Assembly Committee can let the Steering Committee know what is being planned—including ancillary activities—and can request support from the Steering Committee where needed.

5. Have the media subcommittee present an update. The subcommittee working on media coverage can report back on their efforts and solicit advice for further contacts and strategies.

6. Discuss the recruitment of parent and student facilitators by the recruiting committee. The recruiting committee will develop two simple fliers or letters—one for students and one for parents—that explain the purpose of the Days of Respect program and invite recipients to volunteer a set amount of time to participate in the program. Once the recruiting committee has accumulated a list of volunteers (start with more than you will need), they will send each an introductory letter (see the sample letter on page 37). For those who are ready to volunteer, the recruiting committee can follow up with a letter and a packet of information (see page 38).

7. Review the next steps to be taken to implement the program.

Step 5
Conduct a Presentation for Teachers

It is important to inform teachers about the Days of Respect program early on so they will know what will be happening and so those who want to can become involved. The administrative person on the Steering Committee has the important task of defining teacher involvement to be presented to teachers in this meeting. The program is designed to need little teacher participation, but teachers may have valuable experience and ideas to offer. During the meeting with teachers, present an overview of the Days of Respect program, including details about goals, scheduling, and logistics. Let teachers know how they can be involved, such as joining the Steering Committee or working with students on ancillary projects and follow-up activities.

Agenda for the Presentation to Teachers

1. As the organizer, describe the Days of Respect program. A summary of the program and its goals can be handed out at this time (see the sample program descriptions on page 34).

2. Have a teacher, a parent, and a student from the Steering Committee report on the roles each group will play.

3. Have the principal explain the teachers' roles and assignments for the day of the event, as prepared by the administrator on the Steering Committee; e.g. who will be registering or signing in students, who will facilitate groups, and who will monitor the assembly.

4. Explain the logistics of the actual Days of Respect program.

5. Hold a question-and-answer period.

Step 6
Finalize the Plan

Fourth Steering Committee Meeting

The major goals of the fourth Steering Committee meeting are to review every stage and assignment of the Days of Respect program and to finalize any remaining details of the plan.

Agenda for the Fourth Steering Committee Meeting

1. Have the Assembly Committee present a progress report.

2. Have the media subcommittee present a report on their work.

3. Review the progress of the entire program. This planning period is crucial to the success of the entire program. If more time is needed, schedule another meeting before the Steering Committee training.

4. Address any problems that have arisen.

Step 7
Select Students for the Assembly and Small Groups

Meet with the principal and other relevant administrative staff to select the number of students you want for the assembly and the small groups. We recommend approximately 250 students per assembly so that students have a chance to speak in the small groups and to participate fully throughout the morning. The point is not to run students through, or simply expose them to this program, but to actually engage them in it. This takes time and small enough numbers so that students can interact with each other and with the parents and teachers involved.

Your co-organizer or another Steering Committee member can act as liaison with the administration to draw up the student selection and complete the process of notifying all students of the specific assembly and small groups to which they have been assigned. The following is a description of how the selection was done at one school.

Student Selection Plan:

1. On each of the three mornings, approximately one third of the student body (250 students), will participate in the Days of Respect program.

2. These groups of 250 will be selected randomly using the high school computer system.

3. The lists of 250 students for each day will be posted around school well in advance of the training days; students will be responsible for determining their day of attendance and showing up.

4. Students will find the lists of five small groups, 50 students in each group, posted around the lobby when they arrive for the assembly; time should be allotted for students to check the lists.

5. Facilitators will have the lists of the small groups and will take roll at the beginning of the period.

6. Facilitators will accompany their small groups back to the assembly area for the wrap-up and take roll again.

Step 8
Train the Steering Committee

Fifth Steering Committee Meeting

The major goals of the fifth meeting are to train the Steering Committee to lead the small-group exercises and to train the facilitators. Before the meeting, familiarize yourself with the guidelines for training the facilitators (see Step 9 beginning on page 26) and the descriptions of the small-group exercises (see pages 46–51). You don't need to have mastered all the exercises to facilitate the training. This is an opportunity to run through the training agenda, to practice the small-group exercises, to build group cohesion, and to work out interpersonal and logistical problems. The Steering Committee will use the same format to train the facilitators, and they will work with the facilitators during the schoolwide event. At each stage, you and the Steering Committee members will become more fluent with the material and more practiced at facilitating it.

Agenda for the Fifth Steering Committee Meeting

1. Conduct an icebreaker.

2. Train the Steering Committee members to lead the small-group exercises and to train the facilitators. Use the scripts for the small-group exercises on pages 46–51. Allow time for the group to experience each exercise fully (as the facilitators and, ultimately, the students will do). Hold off evaluative discussion of the exercises until the training is over.

   Go over these Ground Rules before conducting the exercises:

   ■ A raised hand means a call for quiet.

   ■ Give the person who is speaking the respect of the entire group's attention.

   ■ Speak your truth from personal experience.

   ■ Everyone has amnesty, meaning that after the workshop no grudges are held between people over what is said, especially by those in a power position.

   ■ ... and any other Ground Rules people wish to add.

   Then, present the exercises (you can modify the order to fit your goals):

   ■ *Dyad Exercise*

   ■ *Stand-Up Exercise*

   ■ *Speak-Out Exercise*

- *Respect Continuum Exercise*

- *Brainstorm Exercise*

3. After the training, allow time for the Steering Committee to reflect on the exercises and to suggest modifications to content or format, which can be tried out at the facilitator training.

4. Have the Assembly Committee report to the group. This will be the final report from the Assembly Committee before the facilitator training, which will contain a run-through of the assembly.

5. Conduct an update on facilitator recruitment.

6. Have the media subcommittee present an update of their efforts.

7. Assign roles for the facilitator training. Distribute the handout on assignments for facilitators (see pages 39–40). Each Steering Committee member should be assigned a role for conducting part of the upcoming facilitator training. Those who are less confident can pair up with more experienced members.

8. Review the next steps.

Step 9
Train Facilitators

In this step the organizers and the Steering Committee train the large group of parents and student volunteers to be exercise leaders for the schoolwide event. The approximately three-hour training will enable the volunteers to lead the small-group exercises with the student body, and to help with other tasks that may be necessary during the actual program. During the training the volunteers will also get to see a dress rehearsal of the Days of Respect assembly so they will know what to expect.

Agenda for the Facilitator Training

Prior to the training, choose several facilitators to be *key facilitators*. Each key facilitator will coordinate a team of five facilitators (including the key facilitator) for each small group. They will assign jobs, record the assignments, and be responsible for handing out job descriptions to the facilitators.

1. Conduct a welcome and introductions. Start with some opening remarks, and then introduce the Steering Committee members and other key personnel.

2. Present an overview of the Days of Respect program.

3. Describe the Days of Respect assembly. After describing the full Days of Respect event, explain that the facilitators' primary responsibility will be to help facilitate the exercises and to assist students wherever needed. Emphasize that they will not be expected to do anything they would feel uncomfortable doing.

4. Ask participants as they go through the training to be aware of tasks they might want to take responsibility for on the day of the assembly. Introduce the key facilitators, and explain their role.

5. Conduct a dress rehearsal of the Days of Respect assembly. Duplicate as much of the actual assembly schedule as possible. By conducting the rehearsal, you will see where difficulties might arise. Take steps to address any potential difficulties before the actual event.

6. Have facilitators break off into groups of 20 to 25 to conduct the exercises. Preassigned Steering Committee members will lead the facilitators in the exercises, in the same order as they were presented before (unless modifications have been made to the exercises).

7. Break facilitators into teams of five, including one key facilitator per group. Distribute the exercise scripts, and have team members choose assignments to facilitate and discuss how they will work together.

8. Regroup facilitators for questions and answers. Allow time for facilitators to volunteer for specific tasks for the schoolwide event.

Step 10
Conduct the Days of Respect Event

The Days of Respect event takes place in three parts:

1. **(1 hour)** The entire student body (or a percentage of it each day, depending on the number of students and the space available) attends a lively, multimedia assembly dealing with the theme of respect as it relates to harassment, racism, sexism, fighting, substance abuse, and other pertinent issues.

2. **(2 hours)** Students gather in heterogeneous groups to engage in the small-group exercises, which are led by student and parent facilitators.

3. **(1/2 hour)** Everyone returns to the large-group assembly hall to take part in an open-microphone wrap-up activity and complete an evaluation form.

See the sample Days of Respect schedule of events on pages 42-43 for a more detailed description of the days' activities, or the revised plan that the Steering Committee has adopted.

Step 11
Hold a Follow-up Meeting and Make Continuation Plans

Schedule a Steering Committee meeting about a week or two after the Days of Respect event. The evaluations should have been completed and summarized and the brainstorming sheets, which were created in the small groups during the Brainstorming Exercise, collected and tabulated prior to this meeting.

The primary goal of the follow-up meeting is to celebrate the success of the Days of Respect program, and it may include a meal or refreshments. This is a time to appreciate and honor the Steering Committee members and others who made the program a success. During the meeting, the group will evaluate the success of various components of the program in order to improve future events, and will review the suggestions that came out of the brainstorming sessions to begin planning follow-up activities.

Agenda for the Follow-up Steering Committee Meeting

1. Conduct congratulations and ask for comments.

2. Summarize the information from the evaluation forms. As a group, briefly discuss each part of the Days of Respect program. Evaluate the success of each component, and note suggestions for ways in which future events can be improved.

3. Summarize the information from the brainstorming sheets. As a group, analyze the patterns of concerns and problem situations within the school. Prioritize the concerns and organize the suggestions so steps can be taken to make changes where necessary. Decide which suggestions can be implemented right away, which can be initiated for longer-term development, and which need further research.

4. Make recommendations as a group for next steps, based upon the student recommendations gathered from the brainstorming sheets. Letters should be drafted to appropriate places of action in the school community, e.g., the student government, the PTA, the school administration, the school board, and campus or community security. The group should decide which recommendations to send to which places, and empower volunteers to complete and send the letters. Acknowledge this as an important moment—the moment of completing the group's responsibilities and of transferring power (of course, particular group members will go on to work in the above-mentioned places to move the process further).

5. Conduct a closing exercise. Go around the group, and have each person choose another person in the group and express appreciation for something that person did or said during the Days of Respect process. Also ask each person to relate something he or she learned from participating in the program. Ask the people receiving appreciation to allow themselves to be acknowledged. Conclude by thanking everyone for their participation.

As organizers, prepare a final report that summarizes what happened during the Days of Respect program, notes the modifications that were made, evaluates how the program went based on the Steering Committee discussion, and makes recommendations to the principal and school board for follow-up to and continuation of the program. Include any documentation or notes that would be helpful to future coordinators. Send the recommendation section of the report to Steering Committee members, media people, and interested community members.

■ ■ ■

At this point, the official Days of Respect program is concluded. The Steering Committee may decide to disband or to continue. Small groups may spin off to pursue specific follow-up activities. Other campus groups may decide to initiate projects or to use the Making the Peace curriculum to continue to address issues of violence in students' lives. Congratulate yourself on a job well done!

From here on, the responsibility for the Days of Respect program has moved from your shoulders to other organizers, the Steering Committee, the Assembly Committee, and to all members of the school community. The next step is democracy in action, with guidance from everyone who has worked on the program. Which of the groups that have formed will continue? What new groups will be formed? How will the event be prepared for and conducted next year? How will the findings from this event be put to work to create concrete change across the campus? How will new students, parents, teachers, and other people be brought into the process?

You will find suggestions for continuation activities in the *Making the Peace* curriculum guide. *But you, the Steering Committee, and the students at your school have the most clear and powerful images of what needs to happen next to make every day a day of respect.*

Handouts, Exercises, Letters, and Surveys

The Ground Rules used by facilitators when working with students in small groups are a subset of the following agreements, which are useful for groups working within a short time span.

1. Respect others   I agree to give everyone respect, including myself. This includes being here—physically and mentally—when everyone else is here.

2. Listen to others   I agree to listen to others and to expect that others will listen to me. One person will talk at a time, without interruptions, and no one will monopolize the conversation.

3. Keep confidentiality   I agree to keep what is said in class or discussions confidential. I won't repeat what someone else says without getting that person's permission.

4. Offer amnesty   I agree not to blame, or "get back at" later, anyone for what he or she says. *Exception:* If someone says that he or she is being hurt now, or is going to hurt someone else or himself or herself, I will try to get that person some help.

5. Use put-ups, not put-downs   I agree not to put down, make fun of, or attack other people. I will not put myself down either; for example, I will not begin speaking by saying something like, "This may sound stupid, but . . . "

6. Avoid crosstalk and piggybacking   I agree to allow everyone to say what they need to say without debating, denying, attacking, *or* agreeing with or supporting it. I will allow people's words to stand on their own, without trying to take them over.

7. Allow the right to pass   I agree that everyone has the right to be silent when they want to be.

8. Respect feelings   I agree to respect and allow other people—and myself—to experience feelings of hurt, sadness, boredom, anger, and excitement.

9. Use "I" Statements   I agree to speak only for myself and my own experiences. I will try to use the word *I* in place of the words *you, we,* or *they*. (This is a very difficult agreement to keep, but crucial. It helps us to speak about what is true for us and understand how each person feels.)

10. Try on the process   I agree to try on the process—these agreements and the ideas in this program—and I realize that in trying it on, I am not required to agree with it or accept it.

11. Take care of myself   I agree, as much as possible, to take charge of my own needs. This includes enjoying and having fun during the process.

. . . and these additional agreements, which the group has decided on:

Dear _____,

Thanks so much for your willingness to be part of the *(your school)* Days of Respect Steering Committee. I hope you will find the time and energy you put into this program rewarding, and will come away feeling you have had a positive impact on the students and the community.

The Steering Committee will be made up of about six teachers, six students, six community members, and the principal and vice principal. The people invited to be on the Committee are:

Students _____

Parents _____

Faculty _____

The Steering Committee's role is to plan and oversee the Days of Respect program and to participate in its implementation. I'm enclosing a description of the project, an outline of the implementation steps, and a sample assembly agenda. When you come to the first meeting, you may already have questions, comments, and suggestions. All input will be helpful, from the broadest issues to the smallest details.

Functions of the Days of Respect Steering Committee

- To refine and approve all aspects of the Days of Respect program, including the assembly presentation
- To attend three or four planning and organizational meetings
- To attend a training to learn to be a facilitator
- To help recruit and help train 20 parents, 30 teachers, and 70 students to be facilitators
- To help with publicity
- To act as facilitators at the Days of Respect event
- To attend an evaluation, recommendation, and celebration meeting

I know your time is valuable, and I will do my best to keep the number of meetings low and the time limit of each meeting to 2½ hours. If things go smoothly, your commitment should involve eight meetings at most, and a half day at the Days of Respect event itself.

The first meeting will be on _____ and will be held at _____.
Because meetings will end in a timely manner, we will begin precisely at _____.
I'll see if I can have some munchies there.

I think we have gathered a wonderful group of people to work on this fulfilling project, and I look forward to seeing you.

Warmly,

Days of Respect is a collaborative, in-school program in which students, parents, and teachers work together to end verbal, emotional, sexual, and physical harassment and abuse on campus through a series of workshops, assemblies, and classroom activities organized around the theme of respect. The program brings young people and adults together to meet, to plan, to train each other, and, finally, to facilitate a multiday Days of Respect event. This event includes a schoolwide assembly featuring skits, videos, and presentations of all kinds illustrating topics that call for respect, like sexual harassment, racial tension, and substance abuse. This is followed by small-group activities and discussion, facilitated by students and parents trained by the steering committee, and culminates in a student speak-out, leading to follow-up plans for addressing campus issues of harassment, abuse, and violence.

The program is designed for junior high, middle, and high schools, private schools and continuation schools, and small colleges with tight budgets and few extra resources. The program can also be adapted and expanded to meet the needs of particular schools.

Days of Respect provides an effective structure to help students, faculty, and parents address problems specific to their particular school. It helps build understanding and mutual regard between the diverse groups that make up a school community—such as groups defined by race, gender, lifestyle, or economic status. Key to the success of the Days of Respect program is the community and coalition building required to design and implement the program. This involves a steering committee of faculty, students, and parents.

Timeline of Events

The entire program takes two to three months and includes these components:

- Four meetings, two to three hours each, of an organizer and a steering committee
- An assembly committee
- One three hour meeting with approximately 120 parents, teachers, and students (depending upon the size of the school) to train them to facilitate the small-group exercises
- One half day involving the entire school community (or, depending upon the size of the school, three half days involving one-third of the student body each day)

Expected Outcomes

- To positively affect the climate of the school
- To improve relationships among school community members
- To gain greater understanding and appreciation of differences
- To prevent violence in all forms
- To generate activities to build school safety and respect

Target Audience

All school community members

Recorder

The recorder takes minutes of the meetings and keeps track of all decisions that the Steering Committee makes.

Media Outreach Facilitator

The media outreach facilitator coordinates the media committee which contacts local media—including newspapers, radio, and television and cable stations—to let them know about the project, and to invite them to participate and cover the Days of Respect program.

Parent Volunteer Coordinator

The parent volunteer coordinator helps keep parents involved and informed about the project and coordinates their participation.

Student Organizer

The student organizer helps keep the students on the assembly committee (and possibly in the Steering Committee as well) involved. The student organizer also helps generate schoolwide support for the program through ancillary activities, such as creating posters and working with already established school committees and community organizations.

Needs Assessment and Evaluation Coordinator

The needs assessment and evaluation coordinator will conduct, or put together a team to conduct, a needs assessment during the initial phase of the program, and an evaluation process at the end of the program.

Assembly Committee and Assembly Presentation Coordinator

This person—preferably a teacher or a drama director—will coordinate the creative student and community components of the Days of Respect assembly.

School Administrator in Charge of Logistics

This school administrator is in charge of organizing student groups and the assembly, and is involved in details such as altering schedules and assigning people to classrooms.

The press release is sent to all local radio, television, and print media alerting them to the exciting violence prevention initiative occurring at your school and inviting their participation and coverage.

Everything must be brief!!!

Lay out the release clearly and succinctly. Include a sentence or two to answer each of the following questions.

- What is the Days of Respect program?
- Why are we doing it? (State the problem, and the goals of the program.)
- Who is involved?
- What are we doing, and when? (Outline the day's activities.)

Also, include the following:

- An explanation of parent/student/teacher collaborative planning and implementation.
- Good visuals (such as photos) and inspirational quotes from adults, students, or faculty, if available.
- A list of articulate and enthusiastic contact people with day and evening phone numbers. (This is critical, as many journalists won't read the information; they will just call the contacts for details.)

Dear Days of Respect Facilitator,

We are glad you will be part of the Days of Respect program. We know you will find the experience interesting, fun, and rewarding. You are one of 30 teachers, 70 students, and 20 parents who will help to facilitate a half-day event to build respect among the students and teachers at our school.

Your *commitment* will be to attend a training on _____, and to attend the Days of Respect event on _____. You will not be asked to take on any more than feels comfortable for you.

At the training session we will watch a run-through of the assembly program, and then break into groups of approximately 25 people each. In these groups, we will receive training and experience the same exercises that will occur on event day.

Finally, we will all return to the main assembly for a closing experience.

At the training, you will find out everything you need to know about the actual event.

If you have any questions, please contact anyone on the Steering Committee. And thank you for your participation!

Warmly,

_____

The Steering Committee

Dear Facilitator,

Many thanks for volunteering to participate in the Days of Respect program. The time and energy you invest in this program will be greatly appreciated and will help to make our school a better place for all our students.

Our goal is to improve the school environment for students, parents, and teachers by having the entire community think and talk about respect and the lack of it. This will improve the way students treat one another at our school, give parents an opportunity to be more closely connected with what goes on here, and give students, parents, and teachers an opportunity to work together to solve community problems.

We have enclosed the following information:

1. "Tasks for Facilitators," a description of what the facilitators will do

2. "Schedule of Events," an outline for what will occur at the schoolwide assembly

3. "Student Selection Process," a description of how students are selected to participate in the small groups and the assemblies

4. A detailed outline of the program activities for the assembly including "Dyad Exercise," "Stand-Up Exercise," "Speak-Out Exercise," "Respect Continuum Exercise," and "Brainstorm Exercise"

5. A "Glossary of Terms"

Please review these materials before the facilitator training on _____ , and bring them with you to the training.

Again, thank you for your help. Working together, we are making our school a place where everyone can feel safe and respected.

Sincerely,

Facilitator's Training

Time _____

Place _____

(Please bring this packet)

Prior to the Assembly

Assemble all the materials (and people) the facilitators will need:

- Attendance lists
- Butcher paper, tape, and markers
- Two people (preferably a parent and student) to arrange chairs in each room. This will require placing at least 35 chairs in a circle in their room, and putting them away.

At the Assembly

Take attendance as students arrive.

Post group lists around the entrance.

Remind students to check posted lists for their group assignment.

Keep track of time during the assembly.

At the Small-Group Meetings

Set up chairs in rooms (if not done already).

Post or write schedule on board for all to see.

Place all necessary materials in the rooms.

In the Small Groups

Two facilitators take attendance.

Two facilitators act as recorders. The recorders will switch off; one recorder will write one statement on butcher paper, and the other will write the next. They will listen to the facilitator telling them what to write, and should probably write the statements using different colors.

One facilitator lays out the Ground Rules. Set them up quickly and efficiently and with *authority*, within the required *five minutes*. The Ground Rules (a subset of the Agreements) are as follows:

- A raised hand means a call for quiet. (Demonstrate.)
- Give the person who is speaking the respect of the entire group's attention.
- Speak your truth from personal experience.
- Amnesty for everyone, meaning that after the workshop no grudges are held between people, especially by those in a power position.
- After laying out the ground rules, the facilitator should ask whether anyone wishes to add any rules. Keep this short.

One facilitator keeps track of time. It is especially important that participants return to the main assembly on time.

One facilitator leads the Dyad Exercise.

One or more student facilitators lead the Stand-Up Exercise.

One facilitator leads the Speak-Out Exercise.

One facilitator leads the Respect Continuum Exercise

One facilitator leads open discussion, asking these or similar questions:

- *How do people get respected or disrespected at our school?*
- *How can we interact in respectful and supportive ways?*

One facilitator leads the Brainstorm Exercise, asking questions like the ones below:

- *What can we do to create an environment in which there is greater self-respect among people at our school?*

At the Wrap-Up Assembly

Accompany students back to the assembly area.

All recorders from small groups post butcher paper from the Brainstorm Exercise in the entrance to the assembly hall.

In General

Help students get to their proper rooms, particularly latecomers.

Add to the discussion, especially if an exercise is moving slowly.

Do what you can to help the program move smoothly and constructively. This is most important considering the tight schedule.

Step	Task	Your Dates	Sample Timetable
Step 1	Present the Days of Respect Idea to Administration and Staff		Week 1
Step 2	Choose Organizers and Create a Steering Committee		Weeks 1–2
Step 3	Conduct Surveys and Create an Assembly Committee		Weeks 2–3
Step 4	Create a Provisional Plan and Begin the Assembly Process		Week 4
Step 5	Conduct a Presentation for Teachers		Week 5
Step 6	Finalize the Plan		Week 6
Step 7	Select Students for the Assembly and Small Groups		Week 7
Step 8	Train the Steering Committee		Week 8
Step 9	Train Facilitators		Week 9
Step 10	Conduct the Days of Respect Event		Week 10
Step 11	Hold a Follow-up Meeting and Make Continuation Plans		Weeks 11–12

Schedule

7:30–8:00	1st Period
8:05–8:35	2nd Period
8:40–9:40	3rd Period — Assembly I
9:45–10:45	3rd Period — Assembly II
	Classes not at the assembly will have an assigned activity
10:45–11:00	Brunch
11:05–12:30	Small-group exercises in classrooms
12:30–1:20	Lunch
1:20–1:30	Return to classrooms and proceed to assembly
1:30–2:15	Closing assembly with everybody

Details: Assembly (a possible scenario)...

1. Students enter with music playing (something appropriate to the topic such as Aretha Franklin's "Respect")

2. Opening welcome and orientation

3. Three vignettes performed by members of the community

Examples:

- Skit with a female and a male student
- Skit with two different cliques
- Skit with a student and teacher

4. Video

5. Personal testimonies

Examples:

- A female student's experience of being harassed
- Pressures on a male student to act a particular way
- Experiences of people of color, people of low(er) economic status, or other groups who experience being discriminated against or treated unequally
- Experiences of mistreatment or discrimination against young people

6. Set students up for small-group exercises

Details: Small group activities (a possible scenario). . .

1.	Set ground rules	5–10 mins.
2.	Introductions: name, class, or where you're from	5–10 mins.
3.	Dyad Exercise	5–10 mins.
4.	Stand-Up Exercise	20 mins.
5.	Dyad Exercise	5–10 mins.
6.	Open Discussion	5–10 mins.
7.	Mini Speak-Out	10 mins.
8.	Respect Continuum	5 mins.
9.	Brainstorm Exercise	15 mins.

. . . then back to large group.

The Wrap-Up will be a large group open-microphone sharing facilitated by _____.

Facilitators should distribute and collect evaluations. Provide pencils as needed.

Goals of the Assembly

- Show a diverse group of students actually leading the process
- Engage all students in the enterprise of building respect
- Set the stage for them to speak out in the follow-up sessions

In general, encourage students to take leadership in putting together the program. Also, remember that the assembly is not a talent show; you do not need to schedule lots of performance time. The performances themselves should not outshine or distract from the other parts of the program.

The Assembly Program

Select individual students to speak to the issues of respect and problem solving at your school by:

- performing a skit
- singing a song or a rap
- reading a poem; telling a personal story
- . . . or any other way they choose to communicate the issues

If a class or group in your school has used the Making the Peace curriculum, there may be students already inspired to express their ideas on this subject. You could also enhance the assembly with participation from school departments:

- the Drama department may have students excited about creating or performing something
- the English department may want to sponsor an essay contest on the subject
- the Art Department may sponsor poster projects
- the Music Department may organize a chorus presentation
- the History or Social Science Department may organize a presentation on how groups of different race, gender, etc., have built or shown respect for each other throughout history

Invite outside speakers, such as:

- parents, grandparents, other family members
- members of the religious community
- police, community organizers
- people from the media
- other local speakers
- . . . or show a short video that speaks to these issues

Choose someone who is effective in speaking to youth and has a powerful experience to relate. Someone who is known to the students is best, but anyone who can generate interest is fine. The combined speaking time should be approximately ten minutes.

Facilitators should be aware of how students are selected for the small groups and for the assemblies. The number of students has been set to ensure that everyone has a chance to speak in the small groups and to participate fully throughout the morning. Students should be picked by computer or some other process at random to ensure some cross-section of grade, gender, age, and racial composition of the whole school.

The point of the process you facilitate is not to run students through or simply expose them to this program, but to actually *engage* them in it. This takes time and small enough numbers that students can interact with each other and with the parents and teachers involved and participate fully throughout the morning.

The lists of students selected for each day of the program will be posted around school well in advance of the training days; students will be responsible for determining their day of attendance and showing up. Students will find the lists of small-group members posted around the lobby when they arrive for the assembly; time is allotted for students to check the lists.

Dyad Exercise

To facilitate this exercise, first introduce yourself. Then, begin by saying the following, in your own words:

> *In a moment, I will ask you all to get up from where you are sitting and find someone you don't know. Try to pick someone who is different from you—a different age, a different gender, a different race, or a different style. Please get up and find that person and get seated again together as quickly as possible, and we will proceed.*

Ask fellow facilitators to pair up with unpaired students for the exercise. When students are settled, begin again:

> *Please face your partner. Relax for a moment, and take a deep breath. (Pause) One person will talk for three minutes while the other listens, and then you will switch roles.*

Give the following directions slowly and precisely so students will be clear about what they are to talk about.

> *Begin by introducing yourself, and then talk about your reactions to the assembly. Name something you liked and something you disliked. Then, talk about a time when you felt disrespected.*

At a time slightly before three minutes, have students switch roles. Be careful not to let this exercise go on too long.

> *Now if you would turn and face the center, we will move on to the next exercise. Thank you.*

To facilitate this exercise, first introduce yourself. Go slowly from the beginning so students have time to pay attention to themselves and notice how they are feeling. Proceed as follows:

Let's begin by getting quiet within ourselves and taking a deep breath. (Pause) In this exercise, I will ask you to stand silently if the statement I read applies to you. Notice any feelings you have as you stand. If you decide not to stand for something that applies to you, think about what you would need to feel safe enough to stand up for that statement. Please do this exercise in silence. If you feel a need to laugh, make comments, or talk, notice what uncomfortable feelings you may be having that these gestures may be trying to cover up.

These statements are addressed to young people; if you are an older person, think of the time when you were in school yourself.

1. Please stand up silently if your dress or appearance was ever criticized or ridiculed by an adult.

(Ask students to notice who is standing and to take note of their own feelings. Then ask everyone to sit down, and proceed slowly with the next statement. Read every statement slowly, allowing time for students to notice who is standing, to notice their own feelings, and then to sit down.)

Please stand up silently if:

2. You have ever been made to feel ashamed or humiliated by a teacher or schoolmate.

3. You were ever ignored, served last, or watched suspiciously in a store because you were a young person.

4. You have ever felt your physical safety threatened or violated at school.

5. You were ever yelled at, commented upon, whistled at, touched, or harassed in a public place.

6. You ever heard degrading jokes, comments, or put-downs about women, people of color, Jews, people with disabilities, or lesbians and gays made in your presence.

7. You were ever the object of slurs, comments, put-downs, or violence due to prejudice.

8. You were ever in a situation in which you felt conspicuous, uncomfortable, or alone because you were the only representative of your racial or ethnic group, gender, or sexual orientation.

9. You have ever received less than full respect, attention, or response from a doctor, police officer, court official, or other professional because of your age, race, gender, sexual orientation, or physical ability.

10. You have ever been hit by an adult or a peer.

This exercise is adapted from *Helping Teens Stop Violence: A Practical Guide for Counselors, Educators, and Parents* by Allan Creighton with Paul Kivel. Alameda, CA: Hunter House, 1992. © 1992 Allan Creighton, Battered Women's Alternatives, and the Oakland Men's Project.

11. You were ever forced to fight or otherwise defend yourself against another student.

12. You ever drank, took other drugs, overate, or did something risky or unsafe in order to cover your feelings or hide the pain.

When students are seated again, proceed:

Turn to your partner, and take turns sharing whatever you are comfortable sharing about the feelings that came up for you during the exercise. You will each have three minutes while the other person listens. Please begin.

After the pairs have finished sharing, say:

Now if you would turn and face the center, we will proceed with group discussion.

This exercise may be facilitated with a "talking stick." In this technique, the person holding a stick (or some other object) talks while everyone else listens. The stick is then passed to another person. Begin the discussion by asking:

Would anyone like to share any feelings or thoughts that came up during the Stand-Up Exercise?

Allow time for everyone who wants to share.

Before the exercise, write these statements on a piece of butcher paper:

One thing I never want to see again is...

We can heal the wounds by...

The facilitator (preferably a teacher) should get students settled down as quickly as possible. You may be running late, and it is important that everyone return on time to the wrap-up of the event.

To facilitate this exercise, first introduce yourself. Then, draw the group's attention to the butcher paper with the pre-written statements:

Anyone who would like to stand up and make a statement to the group that begins with either of the two statements written here, please go ahead. It is not necessary to raise your hand. When you feel ready, please stand up and speak.

One of the other facilitators might want to have an idea ready to offer if the group needs some warming up. As ideas are offered, one of the recorders should write them under the appropriate statement. Allow time for everyone who wants to speak.

Conclude by thanking everyone for their participation in the group, then get the group settled down as quickly as possible.

Respect Continuum Exercise

To facilitate this exercise, first introduce yourself. Then, in your own words, say:

> *We'd like your opinion about how you see respect at our school. Imagine there is a line running across the front of the room.*

Walk along an imaginary line as you continue:

> *This line is a continuum. On this end, there is absolutely no respect given to anyone at our school: teachers and students treat each other with no regard. On this end, there is total respect at our school: individuals treat each other with ultimate respect no matter what the differences are between them. I'd like all of you to get up and stand on a spot on this line that best describes how you feel about the situation at our school.*

This should be done very quickly. Once people have all placed themselves along the continuum, have them quickly sit down again. Allow time for a brief discussion about how students see the situation at their school, then move on to the Brainstorm Exercise.

Before the exercise, write the following question on a piece of butcher paper:

What can we do to create an environment in which there is greater respect among people at our school?

To facilitate this exercise, introduce yourself, and then ask students for suggestions. As suggestions are offered, one of the recorders should write them on the butcher paper.

Conclude the exercise by saying:

Thank you very much. We will take your ideas with us to the assembly for the wrap-up.

The purpose of this survey is to gather information so we can make this school a safer place. Please do not put your name on this survey. The surveys will remain anonymous and confidential.

	not at all	some of the time	most of the time	all of the time
1. Students treat each other with respect at this school.	☐	☐	☐	☐
2. Students treat teachers with respect at this school.	☐	☐	☐	☐
3. Teachers treat students with respect at this school.	☐	☐	☐	☐
4. Teachers treat teachers with respect at this school.	☐	☐	☐	☐
5. I feel a part of school life here.	☐	☐	☐	☐
6. I feel recognized and supported for who I am.	☐	☐	☐	☐
7. I feel comfortable walking through the halls.	☐	☐	☐	☐
8. I feel safe at school. One place I feel unsafe is:	☐	☐	☐	☐

The thing that makes me feel most unsafe is:

9. Students at this school respect ethnic and racial differences.	☐	☐	☐	☐
10. My racial, ethnic, religious, or cultural identity is acknowledged and respected at this school.	☐	☐	☐	☐
11. I have personally experienced ethnic or racial discrimination at this school.	☐	☐	☐	☐

I have experienced the following, or seen these things happen, to others of my ethnic or racial group:

I have contributed to ethnic or racial disrespect by:

	not at all	some of the time	most of the time	all of the time
12. Administrators respect ethnic and racial differences at this school.	☐	☐	☐	☐
13. Teachers respect ethnic and racial differences at this school.	☐	☐	☐	☐
14. Students are respectful of people's sexual orientation (lesbian, gay, heterosexual, bisexual) at this school.	☐	☐	☐	☐
15. This school is safe for students who are lesbian, gay, or bisexual.	☐	☐	☐	☐
16. Male and female students are respectful of each other at this school.	☐	☐	☐	☐
17. Male and female administrators are respectful of each other at this school.	☐	☐	☐	☐
18. Male and female teachers are respectful of each other at this school.	☐	☐	☐	☐
19. Male administrators are respectful of females at this school.	☐	☐	☐	☐
20. Male teachers are respectful of females at this school.	☐	☐	☐	☐
21. Students and faculty are respectful of people with disabilities at this school.	☐	☐	☐	☐

I have seen the following disrespectful behavior:

What grade are you in?

What is your gender?

Is there an adult at this school with whom you feel comfortable talking?

Use the back of this page to comment on any question in the survey. Please elaborate or clarify your answers or add anything else you would like to say.

Teacher Survey

The purpose of this survey is to gather information to help guide the Days of Respect program. Please take a few minutes to answer the following questions. Please do not write your name on this survey. Surveys will remain anonymous and confidential.

	strongly dis-agree	dis-agree	some-what agree	agree	strongly agree
The first four questions are about students.					
1. Most students are well integrated into campus life.	☐	☐	☐	☐	☐
2. Most students treat each other with respect.	☐	☐	☐	☐	☐
3. Most students treat teachers with respect.	☐	☐	☐	☐	☐
4. Special needs students are well integrated in our school.	☐	☐	☐	☐	☐
The next eight questions are about faculty.					
5. I feel like an integrated member of our staff.	☐	☐	☐	☐	☐
6. I am happy to be at this school.	☐	☐	☐	☐	☐
7. Teachers treat their colleagues with respect.	☐	☐	☐	☐	☐
8. Teachers treat students with respect.	☐	☐	☐	☐	☐
9. Administrators treat teachers with respect.	☐	☐	☐	☐	☐
10. I feel supported here.	☐	☐	☐	☐	☐
11. I enjoy being in the teacher's lunchroom at lunch.	☐	☐	☐	☐	☐
12. The humor among the staff is respectful; it is not at the expense of individuals or groups of people	☐	☐	☐	☐	☐
The next four questions are about the entire community.					
13. People accept cultural differences on this campus.	☐	☐	☐	☐	☐
14. People accept differences in sexual orientation (lesbian, gay, heterosexual, bisexual) here.	☐	☐	☐	☐	☐
15. People accept racial differences here.	☐	☐	☐	☐	☐
16. People accept socioeconomic differences here (such as differences in how much money each person has).	☐	☐	☐	☐	☐

Please write a few comments that would help us to understand the atmosphere of the faculty and the student body at this school, including examples of typical incidents if appropriate. Use the back of the page for additional space.

Please do not put your name on this evaluation. Evaluations will remain anonymous and confidential.

1. What day did you attend the Days of Respect event?

For the following questions, please circle the number that best represents your opinion.

2. My experience of the Days of Respect program was

0	1	2	3	4	5	6	7	8	9	10
useless										*extremely valuable*

3. I enjoyed the time I spent at the Days of Respect program.

0	1	2	3	4	5	6	7	8	9	10
not at all										*very much*

4. The program increased my understanding of people who are different from me.

0	1	2	3	4	5	6	7	8	9	10
not at all										*very much*

5. I came away respecting myself and others more than when I began.

0	1	2	3	4	5	6	7	8	9	10
not at all										*very much*

6. I want the issues that came up during the program to continue to be addressed.

0	1	2	3	4	5	6	7	8	9	10
not at all										*very much*

Please write your answers to the next two questions on the back of this paper.

1. Describe two experiences that were significant for you from the Days of Respect program.

2. What would you like to see happen now that would continue some of the things brought up during the program?

Please write any other comments you would like to add.

Following are general definitions for some of the terms used in the Days of Respect program.

Brainstorm Exercise   A quick expression of ideas by anyone or everyone in the group. These are recorded as expressed by group members without much direction by facilitators. No analysis or negative feedback is allowed—every idea is recorded.

Continuum Exercise   A technique for helping participants explore where they stand on a particular subject. The facilitator indicates an imaginary line across a room. One end of the line represents strong agreement with a statement, concept, or opinion that something is a large problem or very prevalent; the other end indicates strong disagreement. An example might be to ask students to find a continuum which runs from 1 (hardly a problem), to 10 (very severe), in answer to the question, "How severe is the problem of harassment at this school?" Students physically move to the point on the line that best represents their belief about the statement or concept.

Facilitator   A person who helps the process to be successful. Facilitators may lead a discussion or activities, encourage the group's involvement, facilitate transitions between activities, and provide a model of participation and leadership for others.

Icebreaker   A beginning exercise for a group to help get people talking with each other and sharing ideas, experiences, or feelings. For ideas and suggestions on icebreakers, two helpful books are *The New Games Book,* ed. Andrew Fleugelman (Garden City, NJ: Doubleday, 1981) and *Energizers and Icebreakers: For All Ages and Stages, by Elizabeth Sabrinsky Foster (Minneapolis, MN: Educational Media, 1989).*

Speak-out   A group exercise in which, one by one, people speak out to the whole group about a personal experience in response to a question or topic.

Stand-up   A facilitator-led exercise in which group members remain silent, but express themselves by standing up when appropriate as the facilitator reads a list of statements.

Talking-stick Discussion   A technique for getting broad participation in a group discussion. The person who has the stick (or other object) talks while everyone else listens. When the speaker is finished, he or she passes the stick to another person who can then talk.

Printed in the USA
CPSIA information can be obtained
at www.ICGtesting.com
JSHW060049150824
68134JS00031B/2681

9 780897 932066